THE CRUSADES

The Fight for the Holy Land

Written by Julie Lorang
Translated by Jessica Foster

THE CRUSADES

KEY INFORMATION

- **When:** 1095-1291.
- **Where:** the Middle East, Constantinople, Egypt and Tunisia.
- **Context:**
    - The expansion of Seljuk Turkish Muslims in the Middle East and Asia Minor, who entered into conflict with the Byzantine Christian Empire and the local Arab populations.
    - Pope Urban II's plan to liberate the Holy Sepulchre, the location of Christ's tomb, which had been occupied by Muslims for several centuries.
- **Key protagonists:**
    - Pope Urban II (1042-1099)
    - Godfrey of Bouillon, first Advocate of the Holy Sepulchre (1061-1100)
    - Saladin, leader of the Muslim troops (1138-1193)
    - Richard the Lionheart, king of England (1157-1199)
    - Frederick II of Hohenstaufen, the Holy Roman Emperor (1194-1250)
    - Louis IX, king of France (1214/5-1270).
- **Impact:**
    - In the East: end of the golden age of Arab civilisation and definitive implementation of Turkish power in the Middle East.
    - In the West: development of Europe and economic and cultural enrichment.

INTRODUCTION

Even today, the eight Crusades led in the Holy Land occupy a particular space in the collective imagination and symbolise the violence of the clash between the Christian West and the Muslim East. These armed pilgrimages, incited by the preaching of Popes and monarchs for almost two centuries, led hundreds of thousands of crusaders to set off, making their mark on history forever.

Far from being limited to a merely religious battle, the Crusades were a political and military conflict between the three great powers of the era: Catholic Europe, the Muslim world and the Orthodox Byzantine Empire. The crusaders managed to seize the Holy Land during the First Crusade and created the Crusader states, small Christian states in Muslim lands whose defence was ensured by the Knights Templar. The expeditions that followed would be vain attempts at reconquering these lands, which, one after the other, were taken back under Islamic rule.

Many well-known figures took part in the Crusades and gained fame through them, including the famous Godfrey of Bouillon, the great Richard the Lionheart and the pious Louis IX. The stories of these great knights are thus intertwined with those of the great battles of Hattin (1187), Damietta (1249) and Al Mansurah (1250). The meeting of these worlds finally allowed the West to catch up in many domains that had been dominated by Arabs until that point, such as algebra, science and philosophy. The major economic and cultural renewal brought by the Crusades would open the doors of the Renaissance to Europe.

CONTEXT

THE BIRTH AND PROGRESSION OF ISLAM

The Muslim world held an important position among the various cultures and religions that were in conflict in the Middle East during the Crusades. Islam, preached by the prophet Muhammad (around 570-632) in Arabia during the 7th century, is therefore a relatively recent monotheist religion, but had already conquered a large part of the known world. Indeed, whether through trading caravans or by force, Muslim doctrine was quickly spreading towards the East – in the direction of Persia and Mesopotamia, up to the Indus River – and towards the West, to the formerly Christian nations of the Ancient Roman Empire.

In just a few years, Syria, Palestine and North Africa were under Muslim influence, thus taking away part of the Byzantine Empire and all of the Neo-Persian Empire (an ancient Iranian dynasty). Constantinople was weakened, but still kept control of Asia Minor – the territory now known as Turkey – and briefly put an end to Muslim ambitions in this region. But nothing seemed to halt the progression of Muslim troops, who took the Atlantic coast and crossed the Strait of Gibraltar to reach Europe at the beginning of the 8th century. After invading Spain in 712 under the command of Tariq ibn Ziyad (died in around 720), they reached the region of Poitiers in France, where they were eventually defeated by Charles Martel (Prince of the Franks, around 688-741).

Bataille de Poitiers, painting by Charles de Steuben, 1837.

As such, in just over a century, the Islamic religion had conquered the East and the South of the Mediterranean Basin, but also a large portion of Asia and Africa. While the Carolingian and Byzantine Empires had stopped Islam in its tracks as it tried to enter Europe, the Muslim world had nonetheless managed to permanently take over certain Christian territories, such as the south of Spain, Egypt and the Middle East.

Muslim civilisation also enjoyed advances in many domains such as arts, literature, science and philosophy, and had its golden age during the first few centuries of Islam. However, its power was weakened by incessant wars between the various dynasties and Muslim caliphates, even though Europe had the advantage of being unified – in the West, around a Pope and soon around Charlemagne (King of the Franks, c. 747-814), made Holy Roman Emperor in 800; and in Constantinople, around the Emperor and the Patriarchate of the Orthodox Church.

At the dawn of the First Crusade, the Seljuk Turks, a dynasty of nomads recently converted to Islam, put an end to Arab caliphates and thereby asserted their domination over the whole Middle East. The arrival of the Turks in the East gave rise to a war between Muslims, but also between Byzantines and Turks due to their expansionist aims. The Seljuks, moreover, were much less accommodating than the Arabs towards Christian populations who had settled or gathered in the Middle East. Geopolitical ambitions, more so than purely religious reasons, were what caused the First Crusade.

THE DECLINE OF THE BYZANTINE EMPIRE

The Byzantine Empire, at that point in decline, also played a significant role in the Crusades. This political power found its origins directly in the Christianised Roman Empire, divided between the two sons of the emperor Theodosius I (347-395) in 395. Honorius (384-423) inherited the Latin Western part, while Arcadius (around 377-408) inherited the Greek-speaking Eastern territories. This split sealed the political and religious destinies of the two entities:

• The Western Roman Empire, whose capital was Rome,

originally extended from the Iberian Peninsula to what is now Croatia, and from England to the coast of North Africa. The Western part did not survive long after the division of the Roman Empire, as it was attacked from all sides by Germanic populations. Emperor Romulus Augustulus (born around 461) abdicated on 4 September 476, definitively putting an end to the Western Roman Empire, which was divided up.

- The Eastern Roman Empire, now also known as the Byzantine Empire, had Constantinople as its capital, and was made up of Greece, Macedonia, Asia Minor, the Middle East and Egypt. Unlike the Western part, the Byzantine Empire did not experience any political or cultural ruptures that could compare to the abdication of Romulus Augustulus, and continued to follow the traditions of the former Roman Empire.

The reign of Justinian I (482-565) and his wife Theodora (around 500-548) marked the peak of the Byzantine Empire's history. The emperor conquered new territories in Italy, North Africa and the south of the Iberian Peninsula, standardised Roman law and built the church of Hagia Sophia, the centre of Eastern Christianity and Byzantine artistic splendour.

The Byzantine Empire began to decline in the 7th century, however, following the expansion of Islam, which deprived it of its rich territories in the Middle East and Egypt. The Empire, which had been reduced to its possessions in Asia Minor, would have to fight against pressure from Muslim troops until the conquest of Constantinople (1453), which marked the fall of the Byzantine Empire. But it did not stop there as, at the beginning of the 11th century, Emperor Alexios I Komnenos (1058-1118) had to contend with Seljuk Turks who had seized the Middle East and were gradually taking over the final territories of the Byzantine Empire. It was in this difficult context that Alexios I asked Pope Urban II for assistance from Christians. Pope Urban II would be the instigator of the First Crusade.

Relations between the Orthodox Byzantine Empire and the West under the command of Rome had not always been harmonious, both for religious and political reasons. The Churches of the East and West had had disagreements due to differing theological interpretations, but the definitive rupture came with the schism of 1054, which separated the two Churches following tensions that affected the Roman papacy and the Constantinople patriarchate. The territorial and political claims of certain popes and Latin monarchs also displeased the Byzantine Empire, who considered themselves the only legitimate heir of the Roman world.

The arrival of the Crusades and the desire of Western knights to appropriate new land and wealth from ancient Byzantine territories revived the tensions between Latin states and the Byzantine Empire, which came to a head with the Sack of Constantinople by the crusaders in 1204.

IN THE NAME OF CHRIST

While the context that led to the Crusades seems to be essentially political, the conflict took on the appearance of a religious war between Christians and Muslims. While most of the Crusades were incited by popes, it is worth remembering that the papacy held a vitally important political position at the time.

In the Middle Ages, the pope was much more than just a religious leader. He tried to create political power for himself through a religion that governed all domains of public and private life. Politicians, conspirators and sometimes supreme pontiffs did not think twice about changing the Christian message – for example, with the promise of eternal life for all those who went to war to liberate Christ's tomb –motivated only by personal interests. These political ambitions could lead to direct conflict between sovereigns, as was the case during the coronation of Charlemagne on 25 December 800, when Pope Leo III (750-816) managed to change the coronation rites so that the emperor had to bow down before him.

Religious power's desire for pre-eminence over secular power could be seen throughout the Crusades, making them a tool which allowed the papacy to resolve numerous problems. Pope Gregory IX (1170-1241) seemed to encourage Emperor Frederick II of Hohenstaufen to undertake the Sixth Crusade simply to keep him away from Italy, so that he could preserve the power of the pontifical states. In any case, despite the undeniable political characteristics of the Crusades, the religious dimension of these conflicts should not be ignored. Indeed, for nearly two centuries, hundreds of thousands of men, women and children set off from Europe to liberate Christ's tomb, hoping that they would thus earn redemption and eternal salvation.

DID YOU KNOW?

The word 'crusade' is derived from the Medieval Latin 'cruciatus', meaning 'marked with a cross', and comes from the fabric cross that the crusaders stitched onto their clothes to publicly show their commitment to the cause.

BIOGRAPHIES

FIRST CRUSADE

Pope Urban II

Pope Urban II consecrating the church of St. Sernin of Toulouse, painting by Antoine Rivalz, 1715.

Pope Urban II was born in Châtillon-sur-Marne (France) in 1042, under the name of Odo of Châtillon or Otho of Lagery, to a noble family in Champagne. Trained as a Benedictine monk, the ambitious young man quickly progressed in his clerical life and was made a canon, then archdeacon of the town of Reims. In around 1073, he became a monk at the abbey of Cluny, but there was another fate in store for him. He was noticed by Pope Gregory VII (between 1015 and 1020-1085), invited to Rome to help with the Gregorian Reforms, and made Bishop of Ostia in 1078. He became a prelate in Germany in 1084 before eventually being elected Pope on 12 March 1088.

Pope Urban II is mostly known for calling for the First Crusade following the appeal of the Byzantine Emperor Alexios I Komnenos, whose empire was being gradually invaded by Seljuk Turks. His impassioned speech during the Council of Clermont (27 November 1095) was what drove hundreds of Christians to set off for Constantinople, then on to Jerusalem.

He died on 29 July 1099, just a few days after Jerusalem was seized by the crusaders. He was beatified in the Catholic Church by Pope Leo XIII (1810-1903).

Godfrey of Bouillon, first Advocate of the Holy Sepulchre

Godfrey of Bouillon treated by an angel, painting by Pierre Mignard, around 1640.

Godfrey of Bouillon was born in around 1061, probably in Baisy, Lower Lorraine (modern-day Belgium) or Boulogne-sur-Mer (France). In 1089 he became the Duke of Lower Lorraine, a stem duchy between France and the Rhine. Godfrey of Bouillon was a fervent Christian and responded to Pope Urban II's call to free Christ's tomb from the Muslim presence, thus becoming one of the main leaders of the First Crusade.

Renowned for his bravery and his humility, he led his men

to capture Jerusalem (15 July 1099) and became the ruler of the newly-founded kingdom. The pious knight rejected the title of king that was offered to him, refusing to wear a golden crown in the same place where Christ had worn a crown of thorns, and thus became the Advocate for the Holy Sepulchre. His reign, however, was very short as he died on 18 July 1100, probably from being poisoned. His brother Baldwin of Boulogne (died in 1118) succeeded him and became the first king of Jerusalem.

THIRD CRUSADE

Saladin, leader of the Muslim troops

Saladin, painting by Cristofano dell'Altissimo, 16th century.

Salah al-Din Yusuf, known as Saladin (name meaning 'righteousness of the faith'), was born in Tikrit (modern-day Iraq) in 1138, but grew up in the service of Imad al-Din Zangi (1085-1146), a Turkish governor in northern Syria.

His glorious military career and the support of his family allowed him to quickly climb the political ladder until he was named vizier ('sultan') of Egypt in 1169. The young man, then aged 31, decided to unify Syria and Egypt, which had, until then, been divided and occupied by crusaders. Emboldened by this unification and calling Arab princes to jihad ('holy war'), Saladin eventually recaptured the city of Jerusalem in 1187. Following this Arab victory, a third Crusade was launched and Saladin had to face the troops of the man who would become his worst enemy: Richard the Lionheart. While the two men were well and truly in competition and fought one another, their relationship had undertones of profound respect. When Richard the Lionheart was unsuccessful in taking Jerusalem, the two men eventually reached an agreement to put an end to the fighting.

Saladin died on 4 March 1193 in Damascus, shortly after the departure of Richard the Lionheart. His exploits, recounted by the crusaders, made him famous in the West.

Richard the Lionheart, king of England

Portrait of Richard the Lionheart.

Richard I was probably born in Beaumont Palace in Oxford, on 8 September 1157. He was the fourth child of Henry II of England (1133-1189) and his wife Eleanor of Aquitaine (1122-1204). As his mother's favourite son, Richard became the heir to the Duchy of Aquitaine and the title of the Count of Poitiers, both owned by Eleanor. Following a series of family arguments and the death of his older brothers, Richard ascended the English throne in 1189 and reigned over the English territories in France: Normandy, Maine and Anjou.

Richard, who grew up in Aquitaine and spoke practically no English, did not stay in his kingdom for long. In fact, the start of his reign coincided with the call to the Third Crusade, which he led. His journey led him first to Sicily, then to Cyprus, where he married Berengaria of Navarre (1163-1230). He then took possession of the island and captured Acre (Israel) on 13 July 1191. Despite these violent attempts, Richard the Lionheart was unable to take Jerusalem and agreed to sign a truce with Saladin.

Richard the Lionheart's return was not easy. After a tumultuous journey, he had to face the conspiracies of his brother, King John of England, known as John Lackland (1167-1216) and of Philip II (1165-1223), king of France, who tried to seize his possessions. Richard the Lionheart thus became involved in a series of conflicts in France against Philip II and died on 6 June 1199, fatally wounded by an arrow during the siege of the castle of Châlus-Chabrol.

SIXTH CRUSADE

Frederick II of Hohenstaufen, emperor of the Holy Roman Empire

Frederick II pictured with his emblem, the eagle.

Frederick II of Hohenstaufen was born on 26 December 1194 in Jesi (a town in Italy), and spent his youth in Sicily, a multicultural land where Norman, Byzantine and Islamic influences mixed. A great lover of culture and a patron, Frederick II invited scholars, poets and philosophers to his court and had a passion for the East.

In 1212 he was made King of the Romans before being proclaimed Holy Roman Emperor in 1220, thus unifying Sicily and the Germanic empire. Although he had been raised by Pope Honorius III (1150-1227) following the death of his parents, Frederick II's relations with the papacy were extremely strained. But Gregory IX, Honorius III's successor, reminded him of the promise he had made during his coronation to go on a crusade. As the emperor was in no rush to fulfil this promise, he would have to be excommunicated by Gregory IX before he finally agreed to leave.

Thanks to his knowledge of the Arabic language and his love of the culture, Frederick II progressed peacefully to Jerusalem where he negotiated the Jaffa treaty with the sultan Al-Kamil (1180-1238), Saladin's nephew, in 1229. In return for promising to remain neutral in the conflicts with other crusader states in the East and to not assist them against the Muslims, he was given Jaffa, Bethlehem, Nazareth and Jerusalem.

When he returned to Italy and the pope lifted his excommunication, the two men nonetheless still had a difficult relationship and Frederick II would even end up being excommunicated a second time following their numerous differences of opinion. The enlightened reign of Frederick II of Hohenstaufen ended with his death, on 13 December 1250.

SEVENTH AND EIGHTH CRUSADES

Louis IX, king of France

Meeting between Innocent IV and Saint Louis in Lyon in 1248, painting by Louis-Jean-François Lagrenée.

Louis IX, better known as Saint Louis, is the final notable figure from the Crusades, but also one of the major sovereigns in French history. Born on 25 April 1214 in Poissy, he was Philip II's grandson, and came to the throne at the age of 12. His reign was inspired by Christian values and was characterised by the wisdom and diplomacy that motivated him.

Louis IX notably conducted a reform and an important development to justice by introducing bailiffs and provosts in his kingdom, and by establishing the presumption of innocence. Some of the laws made during his reign reflect the monarch's wish to lead his subjects to salvation, as is notably the case with forbidding blasphemy, gambling and prostitution.

Following his unexpected recovery from a serious illness, Louis IX swore to go on a crusade, but his two attempts would turn out to be unsuccessful. The Seventh Crusade took him to Egypt, where he was imprisoned, and he died of the plague during the Eighth Crusade in Tunis, on 25 August 1270. Already considered a saint during his life due to his wisdom, Louis IX was canonised by the Catholic Church in 1297 and became Saint Louis of France.

THE CRUSADES

THE FIRST CRUSADE (1096-1099)

Following the appeal for help from the Byzantine Emperor Alexios I Komnenos, Pope Urban II decided to establish an armed pilgrimage with the aim of saving his oppressed Christian brothers and liberating the Holy Sepulchre from Muslim control. In addition to these explicit religious reasons, the pope also hoped to improve the morals of the knights by eradicating violence and private battles between feudal lords. In order to make this idea of a crusade compatible with Christian values, but also to incite people to support his plan, Urban II announced that everyone who left to fight to liberate the Holy Land would earn the salvation of their souls.

Pope Urban II preaching the First Crusade.

The idea of the forgiveness of sins had a big impact in Europe, and Urban II's speech, passed on by preachers such as Peter the Hermit (around 1050-1115) was met with a great deal of enthusiasm by the population. For some, this passion verged on religious fanaticism, and chaos broke out in several towns. Four armies of knights, comprising around 30 000 men, joined the expedition, led by Godfrey of Bouillon, his brother Baldwin of Boulogne (1058-1118) and Bohemond I (Prince of Taranto and Antioch, between 1050 and 1058-1111).

As he was unprepared to see such an army arriving, and fearing for its safety, Alexios I Komnenos helped the crusaders to cross the Bosphorus Strait. On the way, the Christian armies took the towns of Nicaea and then Antioch, before reaching Jerusalem on 7 June 1099. The crusaders besieged the town for 40 days before seizing it on 15 July. Exasperated, the soldiers swarmed into the city and massacred the inhabitants of Jerusalem.

Following this first Christian victory, the conquered territories were organised and shared among the great lords leading the various armies, and became the 'crusader states':

- The County of Edessa went to Baldwin of Boulogne. Created in 1098, it lasted until 1146.
- The Principality of Antioch went to Bohemond I in 1098 and was held until 1268.
- The County of Tripoli went to Raymond of Saint-Gilles (Count of Toulouse, 1042-1105) in 1102 and disappeared in 1288.
- The Kingdom of Jerusalem went to Godfrey of Bouillon in 1099 and lasted until 1291.

DID YOU KNOW?

The Knights Templar was founded at the initiative of the knight Hugues de Payns (around 1070-1136) following the First Crusade, in order to defend the crusader states and the pilgrims travelling to Jerusalem. The military and religious order derived its name from Solomon's temple, located in the Holy City, where its headquarters were based. Recognised by Pope Innocent II (died in 1143) in a papal bull in 1139, the Knights Templar, which had become rich and powerful, was brutally destroyed at the order of King Phillip IV of France (1268-1314), who feared its power.

THE SECOND CRUSADE (1147-1149)

After the crusaders' victory and the establishment of the crusader states, the following crusades would essentially aim to maintain Christian possessions in the Holy Land.

In 1144 the County of Edessa was recaptured by Muslim forces, and Pope Eugene III (around 1090-1153) ordered a new expedition. His appeal was relayed by Bernard of Clairvaux (doctor of the Church, 1090-1153) in Vezelay (Burgundy) and Speyer (Germany). Two sovereigns responded to the appeal: King Louis VII of France (1120-1180) and King Conrad III of Germany (1093-1152). Both led an army made up of 200 000 men from different social classes.

The Crusade was a total failure following a disagreement between the leaders, but also following the many misdemeanours committed by the troops and the poor military organisation of the expedition. Additionally, relations with the Byzantine Empire were jeopardised by the turmoil caused by the crusaders as they passed through the Balkans.

While they were crossing the desert in Anatolia, Conrad III's men were attacked by Turks and massacred in Dorylaeum on 25 October 1147. The German king then decided to turn back, while the Frankish troops continued alone. Louis VII and his men finally gave up on Edessa and besieged the city of Damascus in 1148, unsuccessfully. Following this crushing defeat, the crusaders returned to Europe, without having won a single battle in the East. Bernard of Clairvaux, one of the instigators of this journey, blamed the failure of this Crusade on the number of violent sins committed by the crusaders.

THE THIRD CRUSADE (1189-1192)

Saladin chose to dedicate his life to reconquering the Muslim lands that had been lost almost a century earlier. To do this, he called the Arab princes to jihad and took control of Egypt and Syria. They notably fought in the Battle of Hattin against the forces of the Kingdom of Jerusalem, and eventually recaptured the Holy City on 2 October.

THE BATTLE OF HATTIN

During the battle, the crusaders lost nearly 90% of their troops, or around 15 000 men. After this dreadful defeat, they were no longer able to defend their towns and fortresses, which fell one by one.

The shockwaves were felt in Europe and, once more, Pope Gregory VIII called for a new crusade to liberate the territories that had been lost. More specifically, he asked for help from the Holy Roman Emperor Frederick I (1122-1190), King Phillip II of France and King Richard I of England, which is why the expedition would be nicknamed 'The Kings' Crusade'. But yet again western forces were weakened by tensions between their leaders, as well as tragic accidents that further complicated the situation. During the journey, Frederick I drowned while crossing a river, and his army, the largest in the expedition, ended up dispersing. French troops also deserted the mission following a disagreement between Phillip II and Richard the Lionheart.

After conquering the island of Cyprus, the English monarch managed to recapture the town of Acre in 1191, and had around 3000 Muslim soldiers executed. He then led his army towards Jerusalem, where he met fierce resistance from Saladin's troops. Realising that he would not be able to capture the city, a truce was finally signed between the two men on 2 September 1192. The agreement stipulated that Muslims would keep control of Jerusalem, while allowing Christians to visit on pilgrimages. Moreover, a strip of land between Jaffa and Haifa also returned to the crusaders. Following this agreement, Richard went back to England where he had to contend with the conspiracies of his brother, King John, and his French former ally Phillip II.

THE FOURTH CRUSADE (1202-1204)

Despite the agreements reached between Richard the Lionheart and Saladin, Pope Innocent III decided to launch a fourth Crusade in order to regain control over Jerusalem. While some European sovereigns were reluctant to leave for the East in view of the disastrous results of the two previous crusades, several nobles responded to the pope's appeal: the Counts Louis of Blois (1171-1205), Thibaut of Champagne (1179-1201), Baldwin of Flanders (1171-1205), Duke Odo III (1166-1218) and Boniface of Montferrat (around 1150-1207).

Driven by their desire to find a new way of reaching the East without going through the Byzantine Empire, with whom relations were increasingly bad, the crusaders turned to the Italian republics in order to reach their destination by sea. Venice, through which the troops had to travel, agreed to the journey, but demanded the payment of a significant sum of money (85 000 ducats), which the crusaders struggled to collect. Realising their struggle, the Italian Republic offered them a deal: they would agree to reduce the transit fees if the crusaders captured the town of Zara (modern-day Zadar, Croatia), a former Venetian territory, and deliver it to the Doge. However, the citizens of Zara were Christians, and accepting such a deal would turn the war away from its target of heretics. However, the leaders of the Fourth Crusade accepted the offer and besieged the city (1202). While the citizens escaped alive, the city's riches were pillaged. As soon as he found out about this, Pope Innocent III excommunicated the Venetians and the crusaders for attacking a Christian city.

Despite this punishment, the crusaders continued their journey, but a second deal would definitively distract them from their objective. Boniface of Montferrat, one of the leaders of the expedition, signed a pact with Alexios IV Angelos (around 1182-1204), son of Byzantine Emperor Isaac II Angelos (around 1155-1204), whose power had been usurped. In it, he agreed to reclaim the throne of Byzantium in exchange for the payment of his debts to Venice. While the crusaders were ill-disposed to fighting their Christian brothers yet again, Venice saw it as an excellent opportunity to topple their greatest rival and encouraged the move. The mission was a success and Constantinople was seized in 1203, allowing Alexios IV Angelos to accede to the throne. However, far from being perceived as a liberator, the new Emperor suffered from a bad reputation among the Byzantines, who were not happy about the agreement made between their sovereign and the crusaders. Added to this was the fact that Alexios IV Angelos was unable to pay the crusaders, as the city's funds had been drained by his predecessor. In the end a revolution broke out, and Alexios IV Angelos was toppled from the throne and then killed, while a civil war opposed the Byzantines and the Latin troops. The latter were better armed and left victorious, sacked Constantinople and notably pillaged many works of art. The crusaders then divided the Byzantine territory among themselves and founded several crusader states.

Entry of the Crusaders in Constantinople, painting by Eugène Delacroix, 1840.

Thus concluded the Fourth Crusade which, having completely ignored the power of the pope, had ended up descending into a war between Christians.

THE CHILDREN'S CRUSADE (1212) AND THE FIFTH CRUSADE (1217-1219)

Eight years after the Fourth Crusade, a young shepherd announced that an angel had appeared to him and revealed that only innocent people could deliver Christ's tomb from Muslim occupation. Hundreds of children thus decided to gather in France and Germany to set off on an ill-advised expedition to Jerusalem, despite the warnings of the pope and lords. Unsurprisingly, they met a tragic end: many of them died on the journey while the others were sold into slavery.

The Children's Crusade, painting by Gustave Doré, 1892.

Despite these many failures, Pope Innocent III called for a new crusade and organised the expedition during the Fourth Council of the Lateran (1215), in order to maintain control of his troops. The order was given to Leopold VI (Duke of Austria, 1176-1230), Andrew II (King of Hungary, 1175-1235) and John of Brienne (King of Jerusalem, 1148-1237). The latter quickly took charge of the expedition and decided to attack Egypt to seize its ports, starting with Alexandria and Damietta. His aim was simple: weaken the Muslim forces and negotiate a retreat from Jerusalem. The tactic was promising, and the crusaders besieged Damietta in 1218.

During the siege, Al-Kamil, Saladin's nephew, agreed to begin negotiations and seemed willing to surrender Jerusalem in return for the end of the Siege of Damietta. But a Spanish Benedictine called Pelagio Galvani (around 1165-1230), the religious leader of the Crusade, refused to engage in any discussion with the Muslim enemy and rejected the sultan's offer. The Spaniard's fanaticism drove the crusaders to seize Damietta in November 1219, before setting out on the ill-conceived conquest of the rest of Egypt which, on the other hand, they did not know very well. Trapped by the annual flood of the Nile, they were forced to surrender in 1221 and to give up Damietta in exchange for their freedom.

THE SIXTH CRUSADE (1228-1229)

A few years later, Pope Gregory IX called Frederick II of Hohenstaufen to order, who had promised to go on a crusade against the heretics during his coronation, by excommunicating him. Banished from Western Christian society, Frederick II found himself forced to travel to the East in order to repair his reputation in the eyes of the pope.

He arrived in the Holy Land in 1128, accompanied by a troop of 3000 soldiers. Thanks to his knowledge of Arabic language and culture, Frederick II began negotiations with Al-Kamil, the sultan. After five months, the diplomatic skills of the emperor earned him the signing of the Jaffa treaty. He thus recovered Bethlehem, Nazareth and the Holy Sepulchre of Jerusalem.

The Sixth Crusade was the only one to end without any bloodshed at all, thanks to Frederick II's tact and diplomacy. Rome and the West, however, far from being thrilled at his achievements, believed this agreement signed with heretics to be a scandal. A few years later, Jerusalem was once again seized by Muslim troops.

THE SEVENTH (1248-1254) AND EIGHTH (1270) CRUSADES

The loss of Jerusalem deeply hurt King Louis IX of France, who was extremely pious. After his unexpected recovery from malaria, the sovereign promised to liberate the Holy Land from Muslim occupation once and for all. After lengthy preparations, the monarch set off for Aigues-Mortes, in Provence, along with an army of 35 000 men. After passing through Cyprus, the French troops attacked Damietta once again, which they captured in 1249. They then advanced towards Cairo, but were stopped at Al Mansurah (1250), where they fought hard and left victorious.

The crusaders were exhausted and struck by famine and epidemics, and once again found themselves trapped by the flood of the Nile. The Egyptians intercepted the army in full flight and managed to capture Louis IX on 7 April 1250. At the end of tough negotiations, the monarch was finally freed in exchange for a ransom and the liberation of Damietta. After being freed, the king decided to make a pilgrimage to the Holy Land and stayed in the Frankish towns in Syria for four years. He eventually returned to France in 1254, following the announcement of the death of his mother Blanche of Castile (1188-1252), regent of the kingdom in his absence, who died in December 1252. However, news of this only reached the crusaders in the spring of 1953.

Obsessed by his vow to liberate the Holy Land, Louis IX decided to set off once again for Africa in 1270 and launched the eighth and final Crusade. He set off again with his men to Aigues-Mortes, but this time made his way towards Tunisia, whence he hoped to conquer the East. However, after a few victories, including the capture of Carthage, the crusaders were once more killed off by epidemics and Louis IX died of the plague. The last remaining crusader states disappeared shortly after his death, with the fall of Acre in 1291.

IMPACT

A WORLD CHANGED FOREVER

The crusades were undoubtedly one of the historical events that changed the face of the world. Carried out between the 11th and 13th centuries, they changed the balance of power between the Christian West, the Byzantine Empire and several ethnic groups in the Muslim world, leading to the rise of some civilisations and the decline of others.

For the Byzantine Empire, the crusades sounded the death knell of a long, rich, uninterrupted history that had endured since Antiquity. In two centuries, it had been rendered fragile by constant attacks from the Seljuk Turks, but also by the journeys of crusaders who never thought twice about killing and pillaging, even in Christian lands. The Sack of Constantinople and the formation of crusader states in former Byzantine territory precipitated the fall of the Empire. Weakened and impoverished, Constantinople nonetheless continued to fight against Muslim invasion in Asia Minor until its final capture by the Turks in 1453. When this region of the world finally surrendered to Muslim invasion, the former Byzantine capital became the capital of the Ottoman Empire and was renamed Istanbul.

The Muslim world also experienced a great deal of upheaval and was profoundly changed as a consequence of the Crusades. Indeed, the Crusades ended the dominance of Arab civilisations in the Mediterranean, which had benefited from a considerable lead over the West in many domains, notably due to the use of Indian and Ancient Greek knowledge. The Muslim world was not only attacked by the crusaders, but also occupied by the Seljuk Turks who quickly gained control over it. After the success of the First Crusade, the following Crusades were merely vain attempts to defend the crusader states, which were gradually disappearing. The Turks, however, managed to settle more permanently in the region and ended the Byzantine Empire in 1453 to give rise to the Ottoman Empire. Dominating a large part of the Middle East and North Africa, the Ottoman Empire, far from removing any trace of the Byzantine Empire, actually derived a great deal of inspiration from it. Istanbul therefore has many mosques with majestic domes, directly reproduced from that of the basilica of Hagia Sophia, which has also been transformed into a place for Muslim worship. The powerful Ottoman Empire lasted until the end of World War I (1914-1918) before giving way to the establishment of the Republic of Turkey, which is its direct successor.

NEW KNOWLEDGE

In the West, the Crusades had a positive impact in some extremely varied domains. Although the crusaders had to deal with many failures, the Crusades led to the creation of the crusader states, incredible locations for cultural exchanges and trading with the Muslim world. Thanks to Western presence in the East, the Italian Republics managed to regain control of trade in the Mediterranean, which until then had been monopolised by the Muslims, and became considerably richer. Subsequently, new products were able to reach all of Europe: rice, coffee, dates, apricots, lemons and even sugar and ginger.

These exchanges between the two civilisations also contributed to a flourishing cultural renewal, which would open the gates of the Renaissance to Europe. The Crusades notably allowed Europe to rediscover knowledge from Antiquity, and to measure the wealth of knowledge of the Arab and Indian civilisations in domains as varied as algebra, chemistry and astronomy. The greatest discovery owed to the Arab civilisations was undoubtedly the introduction of their numerical system, which we still use today. These figures gradually replaced Roman notation and were implemented due to their many mathematical advantages, including the notion of zero, which was nonexistent in Ancient Rome.

A FIGHT THAT CONTINUED

Far from ending with the Crusades, the opposition between the Christian West and the Muslim world continued throughout the Middle Ages and the early modern period with the Spanish *Reconquista* (718-1492) and the fight against the Ottoman Empire. While they were finally driven from Spain by the Catholic Monarchs, the Ottomans nonetheless managed to enter Europe on several occasions, notably besieging Vienna in 1529 and 1683. Marked by the fear of Muslim expansion and the myths surrounding some of the great crusader knights, the Crusades now have a significant place in the collective imagination.

SUMMARY

1095
First call to Crusade

1096-1099
First Crusade

1147-1149
Second Crusade

1189-1192
Third Crusade

1202-1204
Fourth Crusade

1212
Children's Crusade

1217-1219
Fifth Crusade

1228-1229
Sixth Crusade

1248-1254
Seventh Crusade

1270
Eighth Crusade

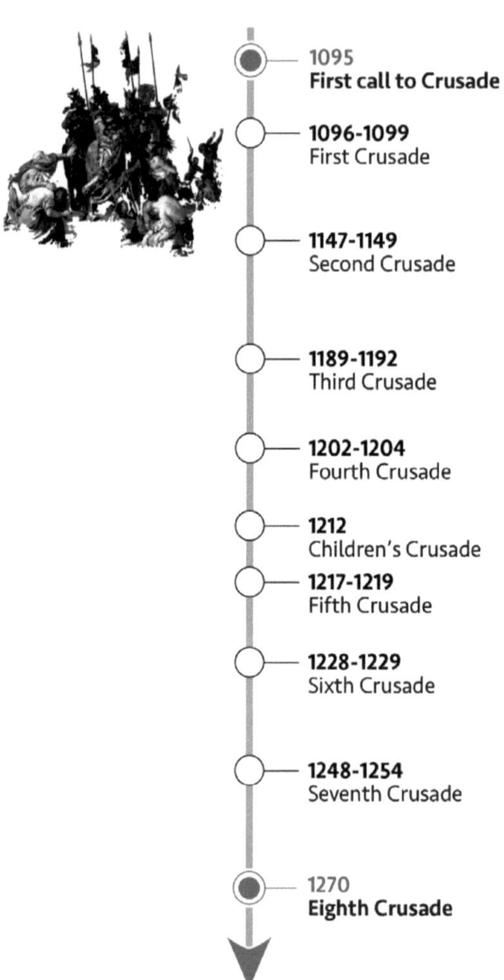

- The eight Crusades were armed pilgrimages which opposed the Christian West and the Muslim East, but also the Orthodox Byzantine Empire from the 11th to the 13th century.
- The first call to a crusade was made in 1095 by Pope Urban II during the Council of Clermont, to free Christian lands from Muslim occupation.
- Although the Crusades seemed to be largely religiously motivated, they also responded to great political tensions between the main powers of the time, notably the balance between secular and religious power.
- Many well-known figures took part in the conflict, the most famous being Godfrey of Bouillon, Richard the Lionheart, Saladin and Louis IX.
- The First Crusade was successful, as it ended with the capture of Jerusalem and the creation of the crusader states, territories occupied by Christians in Muslim lands.
- The following Crusades were vain attempts to defend and recapture these lands, which were gradually reconquered by the Muslims.
- A scandal broke out during the Fourth Crusade when the crusaders, distracted from their objective by the Republic of Venice, pillaged and ransacked Constantinople, a Christian city, in 1204. The tensions between Byzantines and Western Christians, which had been growing throughout the Crusades, reached their peak at that point.
- The Sixth Crusade, led by the Holy Roman Emperor Frederick II of Hohenstaufen, was a diplomatic success: an agreement with the Muslims was reached without any bloodshed.

- The final two Crusades were led by Louis IX, who would go on to become Saint Louis, in Egypt and Tunisia. The French king died in 1270 near Tunis, after catching the plague.
- The last remaining crusader states disappeared shortly after Saint Louis's death, with the fall of Acre in 1291.
- The Crusades had a great impact on the West, leading to economic and cultural renewal in Europe.

We want to hear from you!
Leave a comment on your online library
and share your favourite books on social media!

FURTHER READING

BIBLIOGRAPHY

- Asbridge, T. (2010) *The Crusades: The War for the Holy Land*. London: Simon and Schuster.
- Cazaux, L. (2008) *Au temps des croisades*. Paris: Ellipses.
- Flori, J. (2001) *La guerre sainte: la formation de l'idée de croisade dans l'Occident chrétien*. Paris: Aubier.
- Flori, J. (2001) *Les croisades*. Paris: Éditions Gisserot.
- Flori, J. (2002) *Guerre sainte, Jihad, croisade: violence et religion dans le christianisme et l'islam*. Paris: Seuil.
- Grousset, R. (1981) *L'épopée des croisades*. Verviers: Nouvelles éditions Marabout.
- Heers, J. (1999) *La première croisade : libérer Jérusalem*. Paris: Fayard.
- Hillenbrand, C. (1999) *The Crusades: Islamic Perspectives*. Edinburgh: Edinburgh University Press.
- Maalouf, A. (1984) *The Crusades Through Arab Eyes*. Trans. Rothschild, J. London: Al Saqi Books.
- Madden, T. (2002) *The Crusades: The Essential Readings*. Oxford: Blackwell.
- Madden, T. (2010) *Crusades: Medieval Worlds in Conflict*. Farnham: Ashgate.
- Norwich, J. J. (2013) *A Short History of Byzantium*. London: Penguin Books.
- Richard, J. (1996) *Histoire des croisades*. Paris: Fayard.

ADDITIONAL SOURCES

- Asbridge, T. (2005) *The First Crusade: A New History – The*

Roots of Conflict Between Christianity and Islam. Oxford: Oxford University Press.
- Chazan, R. (1996) *In the Year 1096: The First Crusade and the Jews*. Jerusalem: The Jewish Publication Society.
- Riley-Smith, J. (1990) *The Atlas of the Crusades*. New York: Infobase Publishing.
- Riley-Smith, J. (2014) *The Crusades: A History*. London: Bloomsbury.

ICONOGRAPHIC SOURCES

- *Bataille de Poitiers*, painting by Charles de Steuben, 1837. Royalty-free reproduction picture.
- *Pope Urban II consecrating the church of St. Sernin of Toulouse*, painting by Antoine Rivalz, 1715. Royalty-free reproduction picture.
- *Godfrey of Bouillon treated by an angel*, painting by Pierre Mignard, around 1640. Royalty-free reproduction picture.
- *Portrait of Saladin*, painting by Cristofano dell'Altissimo, 16th century. Royalty-free reproduction picture.
- Portrait of Richard the Lionheart. Royalty-free reproduction picture.
- Frederick II pictured with his emblem, the eagle. Royalty-free reproduction picture.
- *Meeting between Innocent IV and Saint Louis in Lyon in 1248*, painting by Louis-Jean-François Lagrenée. Royalty-free reproduction picture.
- Pope Urban II preaching the First Crusade. Royalty-free reproduction picture.
- *Entry of the Crusaders in Constantinople*, painting by

Eugène Delacroix, 1840. Royalty-free reproduction picture.

- *The Children's Crusade*, painting by Gustave Doré, 1892. Royalty-free reproduction picture.